DISASTERSHOCK

HOW TO COPE WITH THE EMOTIONAL

STRESS OF A MAJOR DISASTER

Brian Gerrard, PhD., Emily Girault, Ph.D., Valerie Appleton, Ed.D.,
Suzanne Giraudo, Ed.D., and Sue Linville Shaffer, Ed.D.

DISASTERSHOCK GLOBAL VOLUNTEER TEAM

As of this writing May 5, 2020 this 70-person team representing 22 different countries volunteered their time to translate Disastershock into 20 different languages and to help distribute Disastershock around the world during the 2020 Covid-19 pandemic. Our team is still growing, and other people are joining the team to expand the reach of this effort. Please continue our work by sharing Disastershock with others and check our website to see how you can help: www.disastershock.com

Olufunke Olufunsho Adegoke - Nigeria
Nyna Amin - South Africa
Parto Aram - USA
Huda Ayyash-Abdo - Lebanon/USA
Liat Ben-Uzi – Israel
Helena Berger - Czechoslovakia
Priti Bhattacharya - India
Sagar Bhattacharya - India
Sandra Sanabria Bohórquez - Colombia/USA
Antoine P. Broustra - USA
Julia Lam Iok Chu - Macau
Andrea Circella - Italy
Alexandre Coimbra - Brazil
Lina Cuartas - Columbia/USA
Sibnath Deb - India
Shuyu Deng - China
Karin Dremel - USA
T.R.A.Devakumar - India
Susanne Ebert-Khosla - USA/Germany
Xinyue Fan – China
Yohko Fick - Japan
Damian Gallegos-Lemos - Ecuador/Spain
Brian Gerrard - Canada
Suzanne Giraudo - USA
Seth Hamlin - USA
Aan Hermawan - Indonesia
Van Van Hoang– Vietnam
Lenka Josifkova - Czechoslovakia
Motoko Katayama - USA
Joanna Wong Pui Kei - Macau
Sheena Kim - USA
Valerie Leong Pou Kio - Macau
Celina Korzeniowski – Argentina
Geliya Kudryavtseva - USA
Amy Lang - USA
Jia Rebecca Li - USA
Akiko Lipton - Japan

Lucía Lemos - Ecuador
Marizela Maciel - USA
Elizabeth Moon - USA
Julie Norton - USA
Sawyer Norton - USA
Yasemin Özkan - Turkey
Kiran Pala - USA
Marie-Claude Parpaglione - Italy/France
Amy Paul - India
David Paul - India
Joseph Puthussery - USA
Barbara Piper-Roelofs - Netherlands
Eliana Ponce de Leon Reeves - USA
Jen Raynes - USA
Andrea Riedmayer - Germany
Karin Rohlfs - Germany/USA
Nihal Sahan   USA
Marie-claude Sannazzari – France
Erwin Schmitt - Germany
Heike Schmitz - Germany/USA
Meryem Danışmaz Sevin – Turkey
Sue Linville Shaffer - USA
Ratnesh Sharma - USA
Jacqueline Shinefield - USA
David Shoup - USA
Alena Skrbkova- USA/Czechoslovakia
Bridget Steed - USA
Zhenrong Su – China
Emilia Suviala - USA/Finland
Ning Tang – Macau
Armin Touserkanian - Iran
Raymond Vercruysse- USA
Justin Wilson - Canada
Yuen Wu - China
Pınar Kütük Yılmaz - Turkey
Philip C. H. Yuen - Macau
Jiayuan Zhang – China
Ruoyun Zhu – China

Dedication

This handbook is dedicated to the memory of Dr. Elizabeth Bigelow, Dr. Larry Palmatier, and Dr. Valerie Appleton who inspired us through their courage, love, and commitment to helping others during moments of crisis.

Cover Photo Credits
    Forest fire photo by Jean Beaufort
    Hands in circle: Adobe stock picture
    Volcano photo by Yosh Ginzu
    Covid-19 photo by Tedward Quinn
    Hurricane photo by FEMA Photo Library
    Flood Photo by Chris Gallagher

ISBN 978-1-952741-23-4

TABLE OF CONTENTS

What Mental Health Experts Say About
DisasterShock: How to Cope with the Emotional Stress of a Major Disaster

"The value of this relatively brief book lies in its comprehensive and down to earth nature. Comprehensive in its coverage of a wide range of strategies to manage emotional stress, as well as its focus on helping children of different ages relax and cope with emotional stress. It is down to earth in that all activities suggested are practical and easy to put into action – especially when you are right there, shocked and tense. A book to have on your shelf for when the unforeseen strikes."

Hans Everts, PhD
Emeritus Professor
Counsellor Education
Faculty of Education
University of Auckland
Auckland, New Zealand

"This is one of the most useful books that I have used in my 28 years as a professor of family therapy and 34 years as a licensed psychotherapist. It is highly informative about the conditions of trauma and its effect on a wide variety of clients. More importantly, it has many useful and effective techniques for minimizing the development of Post-Traumatic Stress Disorder (PTSD) in children and adults. It has stood the test of time because of its utility, and it is an important foundation for training practitioners in the treatment of diverse trauma."

Michael J. Carter, LMFT, PhD
Associate Professor
Department of Special Education & Counseling
Charter College of Education
California State University, Los Angeles
Los Angeles, California

"A must-have resource for disaster management agencies, workers and victims of natural and human catastrophes. A compact manual, it provides practical information for mental and emotional recuperation to cope with the aftermath of life-threatening events and situations."

Nyna Amin, PhD
Associate Professor: Curriculum Studies
University Distinguished Teacher
School of Education
University of KwaZulu-Natal
South Africa

"This is an excellent book and a much needed one as it provides a simple and practical guide to handling emotional shock from disaster. Children are voiceless in time of disaster and the impact can be lifelong. I congratulate the authors for making a difference by sharing their skills and techniques in empowering children and youth."

Professor Cecilia L.W. Chan, Ph.D., R.S.W., J.P.
Si Yuan Chair Professor in Health and Social Work
Chair and Professor:
Department of Social Work and Social Administration
The University of Hong Kong, Hong Kong (SAR)

"Disastershock draws on informed practical interventions for both adults, children and therapists to better navigate the minefield of emotional stress. The book provides many effective tools that can be interwoven into any therapist's existing conceptual framework."

Huda Ayyash-Abdo, PhD
Associate Professor of Psychology
Department of Social Sciences
Lebanese American University
Beirut Campus, Lebanon

"This book (manual) is brilliant in its clarity and simplicity, with easy to follow evidence-based procedures on how parents can immediately help their child/children facing a major disaster. Although addressed specifically to parents, this comprehensive resource is also enormously helpful to professionals involved in providing compassionate care and healing to children experiencing emotional stress especially following a disaster. I will certainly continue to talk about, and recommend, this invaluable resource rich book to my mental health colleagues, friends and family."

Teresita A. Jose, Ph.D., R. Psych.
Psychologist
Calgary, Alberta

"In a simple and sensitive way, the authors of this book supply the readers with tools to help them cope with difficult moments. They give the readers a feeling that they are not alone in this world. Their message is very clear: the authors believe in you! They trust your power to overcome any disaster whether you are an adult, a parent or a child. Therefore, they help the readers to identify responses to disaster shock and encourage the individual to act in order to reduce stress. The authors expose us to variety of stress reduction methods and give us a sense of mastery and control of our life especially in time of crisis. This book conveys a message of optimism: the majority of adults and children can cope with fears and anxieties which follow a disaster. The solution is in our hands! I highly recommend this book as part of our disaster preparatory kit."

Nurit Kaplan Toren, PhD
Associate Professor
Department of Learning, Instruction, and Teacher
Education

Faculty of Education
University of Haifa, Haifa, Israel

"This handbook is an excellent resource for any counsellor or therapist who works with clients who have experienced a major disaster. Although the authors focus on disasters such as terrorist incidents, earthquakes, train or car accidents, I believe this manual can be utilized with lesser fearful or frightening exposure to trauma. Recently in the United Kingdom we have had the Grenfell fire disaster, 'scary clown' social media anxieties, in addition to terrorism in the UK and Europe where children and young people have been exposed to shocking and graphic news reports. This has been difficult for many children and parents.

This is a superb and practical guide with advice and strategies drawn from evidence based theory and practice. I believe this book will help parents, teachers, and counsellors to support children's emotional and psychological resilience. There are clear pragmatic strategies to address the shock to adult witnesses or survivors of a wide range of challenging shocks or disasters. I will be circulating this excellent and informative guide to 300 school based counsellors and 1200 volunteer counsellors all over the United Kingdom and I believe it will be useful to schools parents and counsellors who are confronted by clients who have experienced the trauma of shock or disasters."

Stephen Adams Langley, PhD
Senior Clinical Consultant
Place2Be
London, United Kingdom

PREFACE

We wrote this manual during a disaster we experienced directly: the 1989 Loma Prieta earthquake in the San Francisco bay area. The 6.9 magnitude earthquake occurred during the 1989 World Series in baseball and caused 63 deaths and 3757 injuries. A passenger in a car was killed when a span of the Bay Bridge collapsed. A further 42 persons were killed when the upper span of the Nimitz freeway in Oakland collapsed crushing cars on the lower span. Forty buildings collapsed in Santa Cruz killing 6 persons. In San Francisco 74 buildings were destroyed, fires erupted in different parts of the city, and $13 billion in property damage was done. The emotional shockwaves lasted months. For weeks local and national television showed scenes of the destruction on a continuous basis. For anyone living in California it was difficult not to be deeply affected.

The five authors of this manual were professors and doctoral interns in the Center for Child and Family Development at the University of San Francisco. The Center for Child and Family Development was founded by Brian Gerrard and Emily Girault in order to provide school-based family counseling services for the San Francisco Bay area community. We found that many of the psychological coping resources recommended to adults, and for children, were of a very general nature: get plenty of sleep, listen to your child's feelings, practice deep breathing to relax. However, these general recommendations did not tell the reader how to "listen to your child's feelings" or "how to "practice deep breathing." Disastershock differs from other resources in that is gives explicit instructions on how to lower stress using 20 different practical techniques. The majority of these are cognitive-behavioral and evidence-based techniques known to reduce stress and reduce the effects of trauma.

The manual is in 3 sections. Part 1 provides adults with 10 techniques to lower stress. Part 2 is written for parents, teachers, and anyone working with children and contains 14 techniques for helping children lower their stress. Part 3 contains additional books, videos, and internet resources. We revised Disastershock in: 2001 following the 9/11 disaster in New York; 2017 following terrorist attacks in Brussels, Paris, Lahore, and San Bernardino; in 2020 during the global coronavirus disaster. Through a partnership between the Center for Child and Family Development and the Oxford Symposium in School-Based Family Counseling's Disaster and Crisis Resource Team (DCRT), Disastershock has been distributed free of charge to communities affected by disaster around the world.

We have used these techniques ourselves during disaster and we now offer them to you, not just because we know from research that they work, but because they have helped us personally. Because they worked for us, it doesn't mean they will necessarily work for you. However, they have helped many families to cope with stress. We have listed a wide range of things you might wish to try, to see what works best for you and your children. If you find that using our suggested approaches don't help lower your, or your child's, stress, please consult a qualified mental health professional

INTRODUCTION

All disasters, whether caused by pandemics, terrorist attacks, earthquakes, floods, hurricanes, tornadoes, fires, explosions, volcanoes, tidal waves, airplane or automobile accidents, train wrecks, murder, etc. have one thing in common: Disastershock. Disastershock is the emotional stress that adults and children experience following a disaster.

Those who are killed or injured in a disaster, and their families, are obviously victims of a disaster. Yet the suffering of those who are indirectly affected by a disaster can also be enormous. Disastershock can continue to affect more vulnerable adults and children for up to years following the disaster. This book is intended to help you to reduce disaster-related stress in yourself and in your family members. It is a first aid manual in disaster stress reduction.

Most disasters occur with an unexpected savage force and are over in a short period of time leaving behind devastation and loss of life. However, some disasters are slow moving, like the 2020 global coronavirus pandemic where each day, week and month there are new statistics of infection and death. Disasters remind us of how pitifully helpless human beings can be. Disasters may occur on the global level (2020 coronavirus pandemic), the national level (for example, a terrorist attack intended to affect an entire nation), on a state or city level (for example, when airplane crashes or an earthquake affects a specific geographic area), on a community level (for example, when a neighbor is murdered) or on a personal level (when a family member or friend dies). Whether the disaster is national or personal, those affected experience some disastershock. The worse the disaster, the more people are affected by disastershock.

Some common symptoms of disastershock are:

Jumpiness

Feeling tense

Inability to sleep

Having nightmares

Being startled by sudden noises or vibrations (e.g. a passing truck)

Being afraid to be alone

Worrying about other family members

Forgetting things

Having minor accidents

Crying easily

Feeling numb

Talking more quickly than normal

Avoiding areas similar to where a disaster occurred

Feeling anxious

Feeling angry or irritable

Thinking something terrible is going to happen

Feeling helpless

Feeling guilty about surviving

Re-experiencing earlier traumatic events

If you or a family member is experiencing any of the above symptoms, it is important to know that these symptoms are all normal unless they are severe in intensity or last longer than a few weeks.

This book is intended to help you and your family to cope with disastershock.

Part I describes ten effective methods you and other adults can use to reduce stress.

Part 2 describes stress reduction methods you can use with your children. Although Part 2 was written primarily for parents, teachers and other adults working with children will find it useful.

Most of the approaches described in this manual are evidence-based. That is, they are based on extensive research demonstrating their effectiveness in helping children and adults.

If you or any of your family members are suffering from severe stress, we recommend contacting a qualified mental health professional (such as a psychologist, counselor, family therapist, psychiatrist, or social worker) at once. If the stress coping methods described in this book do not lower your stress (or the stress of your family members), you should consult a qualified mental health professional for more specialized advice that takes into account your unique situation.

PART 1: TEN WAYS TO COPE WITH DISASTERSHOCK

If you are suffering from any of the symptoms of Disastershock described in the Introduction, you may wish to try several of the ten stress reduction methods listed in this section. We recommend that you select two or three methods that appeal to you most, and practice them several times a day. For most of these methods to work, you must practice them each time you start to feel stressed.

Method 1: Deep Breathing

This is the procedure of reducing tension in your body through practicing slow, deep breathing. This is a method you can use any time you feel tense or anxious. It is best practiced sitting or lying where you will not be disturbed. If you feel uncomfortable at any time, stop the exercise.

Let's try it.

Take a slow, deep breath through your nose for two seconds: 1 - 2.

Now hold your breath for two seconds: 1 - 2 and let it out slowly through your nose for two seconds: 1 - 2.

Now repeat, breathe in for two seconds: 1 - 2, hold for two seconds: 1 - 2, breathe out for two seconds: 1 - 2.

Now go to three seconds: Breathe in: 1 - 2 -3. Hold: 1 - 2 - 3. Breathe out: 1 - 2 - 3. Now repeat: breathe in: 1 - 2 - 3. Hold: 1 - 2 - 3. Breathe out 1 - 2 - 3. Now continue deep breathing with a 3 second interval until it feels comfortable.

When you feel ready go to 4 seconds. Breathe in 1-2-3-4. Hold 1-2-3-4. Breathe out 1-2-3-4. Now repeat: Breathe in: 1 2-3-4. Hold 1-2-3-4. Breathe out: 1-2-3-4. That's excellent.

When you feel ready, try 5 seconds.

You should now be breathing slowly and deeply. If you wish, you may extend your breathing intervals to 6, 7, 8, 9 or 10 seconds. Remember to stop if you feel uncomfortable at <u>any</u> time. Practice this deep breathing for at least 5 minutes. You can use this method whenever you feel tense - when you are alone or in public.

Method 2: Brief Muscle Relaxation

This stress-reduction method works by getting you to tense up all your major muscle groups at once for ten seconds, then suddenly relax them. Begin by practicing this when you are sitting alone. Do not practice this while driving.

Let's try it. Are you sitting comfortably? OK, here goes:

Make a fist with each of your hands and squeeze your fingers together tight... tight... tight.... Place your fists against the outside of your thighs and push in so that you are squeezing your knees together. Push, push, push.

Squeeze your eyes shut tight and squeeze your lips together. Suck in your stomach and hold it, tight... tight....

Now press your knees and legs together as hard as you can. Hold all your muscles tight for 5 more seconds 1,2,3,4,5.

Now relax. Let all your muscles go completely limp. Let yourself be like a rag doll. Notice the contrast in how your muscles feel. Notice the sense of warmth and calmness spreading through your body.

Now try it again. Make a fist with each of your hands and squeeze your fingers together tight... tight... tight...

Place your fists against the outside of your thighs and push in so that you are squeezing your knees together. Push, push, push. Squeeze your eyes shut tight and squeeze your lips together. Suck in your stomach and hold it, tight-tight....
Now press your legs together as hard as you can. Hold all your muscles tight for 5 more seconds: 1,2,3,4,

Now relax. Let all your muscles go completely limp. As you do so take a slow deep breath, hold it and let it out slowly. Think the word CALM to yourself. Let yourself be like a rag doll. Continue to breathe slowly and deeply as you notice the sense of warmth and calmness spreading through your body.

You may find it helpful combining this method with Method 1: Deep Breathing. You can use this method-to relax when you are alone or in public (but not when you are driving).

Method 3: Monitoring Stressors and Your Stress Level

This method involves accurately identifying the things that are causing you stress (we call these "stressors") and keeping track of the degree to which you are experiencing stress. If you don't know that you are feeling stressed, then you won't know when to practice your stress reduction methods. If you don't know exactly what is stressing you, you won't know where to direct your stress-reduction methods.

Let's start with stressors. Some common stressors caused by disasters are:

Daily reports on the numbers of persons who are sick or died.

Not feeing safe to leave your home.

Pictures of damaged buildings.

Hospital and ambulance pictures of the sick and injured.

Reading about about how people died.

Seeing homes on fire or being destroyed.

Thinking where you live is not safe.

Not knowing where other family members are.

These are only a few stressors that might be affecting you. A stressor may be something you see or something you just think about. Whatever it is, it triggers your stress. If you find yourself feeling tense or anxious, try to identify the stressor triggering your stress reaction.
Did you just watch the news and see a picture of damaged property? Are you thinking about the victims? Once you know the source of your stress you can bring into action specific stress-reduction methods to lower your stress.

Next, identify how stressed you are. If you are not aware of any feelings, look at your behavior. Are you forgetting things, acting irritable, having trouble sleeping, can't sit still?

These are signs of stress. Try to develop an awareness of your feelings: are you feeling numb, depressed, sad, afraid, helpless, angry, or guilty. Label your feelings. See if you can connect your feelings with a specific stressor (for example, an image of a damaged building). It helps you to understand your feelings when you identify the stressors that trigger your feelings.

Rate your tension level using a I to 10 scale. Make 10 the most tense you have ever felt, and I the most relaxed you have ever felt. What is your tension rating right now? Keep track of your stress levels by rating your tension level several times during the day. Notice the times when your tension level goes up, and use some of the other stress reduction methods to bring it down.

Method 4: Thought-stopping

This is a method for shutting off unpleasant thoughts and images. You can use this approach when you keep having an unpleasant thought or image over and over. For example, if you keep thinking about a place where someone died and you can't seem to turn the thought off, then you might find this method helpful.

Let's try it.

While you are thinking of your unpleasant thought or image, pinch yourself lightly on the arm and think the word STOP!

Take a deep breath and, as you slowly let it out, think the word CALM and imagine yourself in the most peaceful scene you can think of (for example, lying on the beach, resting at the mountains or the lake, or relaxing in your backyard).

For at least 20 seconds imagine your peaceful scene in as much detail as you can.

Concentrate on imagining the scene of beauty about you.

Let your body develop a sense of relaxation as you breathe slowly and deeply. (See Method 2: Deep Breathing.)

For this method to work, you must use it *every time*, repeat: every time you start to experience the unwanted thought or image. The method works by interrupting the unpleasant thoughts or images and by replacing them with positive images.

Whenever you find yourself using a negative label, search for a positive one. The principle is: Every cloud has a silver lining. Look for it until you find it!

Method 5: Relabeling

Relabeling is the method of using positive words or labels to describe something you have been labeling in a negative way. Instead of saying: "The glass is half-empty" you say "The glass is half full." You look for the Positives in a situation and emphasize them. This will help to reduce your stress. For example, if you see a picture of a damaged building, instead of using negative labels such as:

"This is awful."

"So many died there."

"This is horrible."

Search for positive labels:

"There were so many courageous volunteers."

"Not that many died compared to what was first expected."

"Think of the many lives that were saved."

"The heroic rescues of many persons."

Similarly, when thinking about the disaster overall, use positive labels:

"Comparatively speaking there were fewer deaths than was feared."

"Most buildings were not damaged."

"We can learn from this disaster to _____."

Method 6: Positive Self-Talk

This is the method of thinking *Positive Coping Statements* to yourself before, during, and after your encounter with a stressor.
Here's how it works. Let's suppose you know you are going to see something that really stresses you - for example, you have to drive to work and you get very stressed whenever you pass over a bridge that you fantasize will collapse.

To use Positive Self-Talk, make a list of some positive things you can think to yourself before you drive over the bridge, while you are actually on the bridge, and after you have passed over the bridge.

For example, as you approach the bridge you could think:

"There is the bridge, but I can handle it."

"Everything is going to be alright."

"I can manage my stress by breathing slowly and deeply."

"I've handled this successfully before."

While you are on the bridge you could think:

"I can handle it."

"I'll be over in a few seconds."

"Relax and breathe deeply."

"I can stay calm."

"Everything will be alright."

After you have passed over the bridge, you can think:

"Congratulations!"

"I did an excellent job."

"I managed my stress."

"I did my breathing well"

You will find it helpful if you prepare these Positive Coping Statements and then concentrate on thinking them in advance. Concentrate as you go through the 3 stages of encountering a stressor: before, during, after. This method works by interrupting the flow of negative images and thoughts that you might be having as you encounter your stressor. You can use Positive Self-Talk with any stressor you have to encounter directly (for example, passing a spot where someone died or having to enter a grocery store where there are other people during a pandemic).

Method 7: Positive Imagery

Positive imagery refers to imagining doing something that is very pleasant. This interrupts negative images and thoughts that stress you. If you are feeling generally stressed, you may wish to *Fantasize Having a Mini-vacation*. (Don't try this if you are driving.)

Let's try it. Imagine you are on holiday in your favorite vacation spot. If you are at the beach, feel the warmth of the sun on your skin, sense the warmth of the sand beneath your beach towel, feel the breeze gently blowing across your body, listen to the waves gently splashing. Try to experience being there through all your senses. Continue this for about 5 minutes.

If you have to pass by a stressor directly (such as crossing a bridge or passing by a damaged building), try imagining yourself doing something pleasant that involves movement. Imagine yourself jogging; visualize yourself carrying a football and making for the goal line; imagine skiing on a field of snow and notice the snow spraying up over the tips of your skis as you make your turns.

This method works by focusing your imagination on re-experiencing in detail some pleasant activity.

Method 8: Challenging Irrational Beliefs

This is the method of writing down beliefs about the disaster that you think are irrational (but which you still believe) and then challenging these irrational beliefs by finding rational beliefs that contradict them.

Some common irrational beliefs you might have are:

"My family member will get sick and die"

"The highway bridge is going to drop on me."

"Another disaster will occur tomorrow."

"My house is going to collapse."

"I'm going to be killed."

"I am surrounded by nothing but horror."

These are all examples of irrational beliefs because they tend to catastrophize and overemphasize a negative point of view, and ignore positive information.

Give it a try.

Identify any belief you might have about the disaster that you think is irrational or excessively negative.

Write it down on a piece of paper under the heading: Irrational Beliefs.

To the right write the heading Rational Beliefs.

Under Rational Beliefs try to write out some more positive, rational beliefs about the situation.

For example,

Instead of: "My family member will get sick and die."

Write: "If my family member does get sick, they might recover and be fine."

Instead of: "The bridge is going to collapse."

Write: "The chances of any bridge collapsing under me (or anyone) are very remote, there was only 1 bridge that collapsed in the disaster."

Instead of: "A huge flood (fire, earthquake, etc.) will occur tomorrow."

Write: "A huge flood (fire, earthquake, etc.) may just as likely not occur tomorrow. The last time a disaster like this occurred was 20 years ago."

Instead of: "I am surrounded by horrors."

Write: "It is true that many have died and much property has been damaged; it is also true that I am alive and there is much of life to appreciate; this is a very special community and I can be proud of how its citizens are courageous and loving in helping each other."

The heart of this method lies not in glossing over negatives, but in seeing the truth: that in reality there are positives even in the most tragic of circumstances.

Method 9: Restoring Positives/Reducing Negatives

When we are caught up in dealing with a crisis, it is easy to forget to continue doing those pleasurable activities that naturally reduce our stress. For us these include: eating take-out, playing tennis, lying in a lawn chair in the sun in the backyard, watching a favorite TV show; playing with our dogs and cats, listening to music, watching football and baseball, and enjoying the company of family and good friends, to name a few.

You may find it helpful to identify relaxing activities you used to do before the disaster and then force yourself to start doing them once again. By re-engaging in these pleasant activities you will be interrupting the flow of negative images and thoughts caused by the earthquake and you will be reminding yourself that disaster is only a very small part of life.

In addition to restoring positives to your life, you may find it helpful to reduce the negatives. If you feel stressed by pictures of disaster damage, don't look at them right now. Turn off the portion of the news that shows disaster damage. Don't look at unpleasant pictures on the internet. For the time being listen to some music rather than the news. Don't take in more negative images and information than you can handle. If there are unpleasant people in your life that you can avoid right now, avoid them. Identify negative persons and things that depress you and reduce your contact with them for the time being.

Method 10: Developing a Sense of Mastery Through Action

An important source of stress caused by a disaster is the feeling of helplessness it produces in most of us. A disaster strikes without warning and we have no control. There are, however, some things you can do to reduce stress caused by feelings of helplessness. These are activities that you do to develop a sense of mastery or control over yourself and your environment with respect to dealing with disasters.

First, you can develop a *Disaster Preparedness Kit* for yourself and your family (if your disaster was one that knocked out electricity and other basic services). These contain materials such as water, food, a battery-operated radio, flashlight, first-aid kit, blankets, and a written plan describing how family members - if separated - will get in touch. You might want to keep one of these kits in your house and also in your car. In dealing with a pandemic like the 2020 Coronavirus having hand sanitizer, disinfectant, and surgical masks that can be used to protect family members is critical. Being prepared in this fashion will reduce your sense of helplessness. You will know that if another disaster occurs, you have basic survival materials to protect your family and yourself.

Second, you can volunteer to help those affected by the disaster. You could give a homeless family temporary quarters if you have a spare room. You could give blood to the Red Cross. You could donate food, clothing, or money to a community agency helping survivors. Any of these volunteer activities will give you a sense of mastery over the disaster by giving you the sense that you are reducing its negative effects on others. On a more personal front, you can check in with friends and extended family members (using mail, email, phone, or video conferencing) to let them know you are there to support them.

Third, you can become an expert on disasters and disaster survival by reading all you can on disasters. For example, for persons coping with earthquakes, one book we like is called Peace of Mind in Earthquake Country. Knowing about earthquakes if you live in an earthquake prone state can reduce your sense of helplessness. For example, during an earthquake should you stay inside a building or try and get out in the open? Where is the safest place to stay during a tornado? Finding the answers to questions like these will help you build a sense of mastery.

Finally, we recommend you become an expert in stress reduction as this will give you a sense of mastery over your feelings and tensions. There are many fine books on stress reduction such as:

Blonna, Richard (2011). *Coping with Stress in a Changing World*. New York, NY: McGraw-Hill Education.

Burns, David (2008). *Feeling Good: The New Mood Therapy*. New York, NY: Harper.

Chen, David (2016). *Stress Management and Prevention: Applications to Daily Life* *3rd Edition*. New York, NY: Routledge.

Davis, Martha; Eshelman, Elizabeth and McKay, Matthew (2008). *The Relaxation and Stress Reduction Workbook.* Oakland, CA: New Harbinger Publications.

Frakes, Mary (1999). *Mindwalks: 100 easy ways to relieve stress, stay motivated and nourish your soul.* Cambridge, Mass: Life Lessons.

Ricks, Jeanne (2014). *Be More ~ Stress-less! - The Workbook: Realize your best life by retooling your stress.* Nu Day Perspectives.

We recommend that you try several of the above ten stress reduction methods, and try them more than once. If you find that these methods do not reduce your stress and that you are experiencing very high levels of stress, we strongly recommend that you seek counseling from a qualified mental health professional.

PART 2: HOW TO HELP YOUR CHILD COPE WITH DISASTERSHOCK

How to Identify When Your Child Is Stressed

What is stress? It is a reaction of mind and body to particular unsettling experiences. Many stress feelings and reactions are shared in common by people of all ages. Children's stress responses in the event of a disaster may be obvious or subtle. Special attention is required to identify and meet the needs of children.

The most common reaction by children to a disaster is fear and anxiety. A child is fearful of a reoccurrence of the disaster. Another common fear is that the child or a family member might suffer injury in a reoccurrence. Another fear is that the child may be afraid of being separated from the family and left alone. At a time like this it is important for the family to remain together. If your child is unduly stressed by family members being in different places, which is normal in everyday life, the child will be more reassured if you let the child know where you are going to be, whether it is at work or at the grocery store. You should consider using internet video (e.g. FaceTime) to connect with family that is out of the area. Another step to alleviate a child's anxiety is to rehearse what the family members might do in the event that there is another disaster. What are some safety precautions the family will take at home? Identify a plan if the disaster occurs when the child is at school. Who will pick your child up?

During a disaster, parents are stressed too. The parents' fears and anxieties are passed on to the children. An adult has more experience in coping with such stress, whereas children often do not. Therefore, it is important for the parent to recognize the emotional needs of the child. Your child may be scared and frightened. This anxiety often does not disappear by itself. You need to acknowledge with the child that the fear and anxiety are very real. You need to understand what the specific fears are. The only way to find this out is to talk to your child.

Listen to what your child's specific fears are. Talk to your child about his or her feelings. Find out what your child thinks has happened. Your child may have been inundated with television and radio reports, which may have blown the crisis out of proportion. You need to sit down and talk about the facts of the disaster. Continue to listen to the child because he or she will express either directly or indirectly fears associated with the disaster. The most important responses to a child that you can make are to listen, to encourage the child to communicate and to continually reassure the child verbally as well as with extra hugs and attention.

More specific reactions to a disaster have been identified that children of all ages might experience. Immediately following a disaster, sleep disturbance and night terrors are common. Other children may experience a loss of interest in school. This reaction may range from fear of separation, to the anxiety that the school is not safe, to a lethargic response to school activities and peer interaction. It is even more challenging when school is only on-line and communication with teachers is by video only or not at all. Another common response seen in children of all ages is regressive behavior. A child might revert to prior behaviors exhibited at an earlier developmental stage because it might seem more safe and protected. The present situation is unsettling so the escape to a previous secure state is reassuring. These responses are common but such behaviors should not persist for a long period of time following the disaster.

Children of different age groups have specific stress reactions to a disaster. A child who is 5 experiences different vulnerabilities than does a child of 14. For the purpose of this book, the age groups will be divided into Preschool (ages 1-5); Early Childhood (ages 5 -11); Preadolescent (ages 11 - 14); and Adolescent (ages 14 -18). Table I summarizes the most common stress responses for the different age groups.

Children in the Preschool age group (ages 1 - 5) are particularly vulnerable to the disruption of their safe and secure environment. Their development has not reached a level of conceptualization that permits them to understand a disaster. Preschoolers lack the verbal skills to communicate their fears and anxieties. As a result, a Preschooler's stress is best identified by exhibited behaviors. These behaviors may be indirect so special attention to the child's needs is important. Typical regressive responses which are considered normal are thumbsucking and bedwetting. A 5 year old may have stopped sucking his thumb at age 3 and spontaneously begin this behavior again. This is normal but should not continue indefinitely. Another response is a fear of the dark and nightmares. This is particularly heightened immediately following the disaster .It is also tied in with the Preschooler's fear of being alone and this fear increases at nighttime. The Preschooler might exhibit a behavioral response such as an increase in clinging to the parents.

Table 1. COMMON STRESS RESPONSES OF CHILDREN TO DISASTER

Common Stress Responses of Children (all age groups)
Fear of recurrence of the disaster
Fear of injury
Fear of separation
Fear of being alone
Sleep disturbances
Night terrors
Loss of interest in school
Loss of interest in peers
Regressive behavior
Physical symptoms (headaches, stomach aches)
Isolation
Sadness

Stress Responses of Preschool Children (ages 1-5)
Thumbsucking
Bedwetting

Fear of the dark
Night terrors
Increased clinging
Expressive language difficulties
Loss of appetite
Loss of bladder and bowel control

Stress responses of Early Childhood (age 5-11)
Whining
Clinging
Separation anxiety
Fear of the dark
Nightmares
Avoidance of school
Poor concentration
Increased aggressiveness
Withdrawal from peers

Stress Responses of the Preadolescent (ages 11-14)
Appetite difficulties
Headaches
Stomach aches
Psychosomatic complaints
Sleep difficulties
Nightmares
Loss of interest in school
Loss of interest in peer group
Increased rebellion at home
Aggressive behavior

Stress responses of Adolescents (age 14-18)
Headaches
Stomach aches
Psychosomatic complaints
Appetite disturbance
Sleep disturbance
Decrease in energy level
"Irresponsible" behavior
Increased dependence on parent
Withdrawal from peer group
School problems

In the stress responses of the Preschooler (ages 1-5), a disaster increases the child's separation anxiety. Another stress symptom is speech difficulties. Language is a relatively new developmental milestone and may suffer in ways such as stuttering, stammering and difficulty in expressing in a fully coherent manner. A Preschooler's loss of appetite is another stress signal. Loss of bladder or bowel control, particularly in the older Preschooler, will often indicate stress. The overriding anxiety among Preschoolers is fear of abandonment and fear of being alone.

The Early Childhood (ages 5 - 11) group's stress responses are more generally indicated by regressive behavior. Behaviors such as excessive whining and clinging to the parent are common. This group may have an increase in separation anxiety from the parent which is more typical behavior of a Preschool child. The 5 to 11 year old may begin to experience a fear of the dark and nightmares. The nightmares may be connected to past events of the disaster as well as fear of future occurrences. Many stress behaviors are exhibited at school. This child may want to avoid school and even if encouraged to attend school may lose interest and have relatively poor concentration in school. These symptoms should also be brought to the attention of the teacher so the parent and teacher together can effectively address the child's stress. This also applies to on-line school during the disaster. Other behavioral signs range from an increased aggressiveness to a withdrawal from friends and family. In order to determine these stress signals, the parent must try to recall what the child's normal behavior patterns were prior to the disaster. In this way the deviation from the norm can be assessed because each child's so-called "normal" behavior is different. What might be observed as a stress signal for one child is not necessarily true for the next child.

The stress reactions in the Preadolescent (ages 11 - 14) include behavioral differences as well as physical responses. Physical symptoms that signal stress are complaints of headaches, stomach aches, vague aches and pains and psychosomatic complaints. The Preadolescent may have difficulty sleeping and wake up with nightmares. Another physical symptom might be loss of appetite. In a Preadolescent child, the physical symptoms may be coupled with school problems. The child may complain of a headache in the morning and stay away from school. This could also be symptomatic of loss of interest in school and withdrawal from peers, which is also a normal stress reaction. Other children will express stress signals in a more aggressive way. These behaviors include increased rebellion at home and refusal to participate in family activities. Reactions to peers are particularly significant with the preadolescent and range from withdrawal to aggressive behavior with friends. It is important to help the preadolescent by affirming that the physical and behavior responses are normal and shared by other people, particularly his or her peers.

The Adolescent (ages 14 - 18) stress responses also include physical and behavioral signals but this age group's stress is increased because they are caught in the middle (between being viewed as children who need to be attended to and as adults who can cope on their own). The Adolescent is not an adult but an older child who has special needs, as do the other age groups.

Physical responses include headaches, stomach aches, and possible psychosomatic complaints, such as rashes. Appetite and sleep disturbances are also common. Another symptom might be a decrease in energy level where the once energetic and enthusiastic Adolescent becomes apathetic and disinterested in previously satisfying activities.

Behavioral stress responses often show up in the Adolescent's interaction with peers because peers are central to this developmental stage. If the child's school is temporarily or even permanently closed due to disaster damage, this can have a profound stress effect that must be identified and directly addressed. Other behavioral stress responses might be irresponsible behavior - a "nothing can affect me" attitude, or dependent behavior at the other end of the spectrum where the Adolescent becomes less independent and tends to cling more to the family. It is most important to listen and talk to the Adolescent and try to reconnect the child with his or her peer group.

The most important way to determine the child's stress reactions in any age group is to listen to the child's fears and anxieties. Although these fears may seem childish or insignificant to an adult they are very real to the child. If your child is one who is shy about communicating then you may have to initiate the discussion. Parents' love, hugs, and extra attention are important ways to help children to cope with a stressful situation. A disaster is not a situation where we can say it's permanently over. We must live with the possibility of another disaster, as well as continue to live with the ramifications of the original disaster, whether it is the closing of a school, rebuilding of a home or disruption of traffic patterns. The effects don't disappear immediately.

It is important to note that the majority of children will cope and overcome the fears and anxieties of a disaster. But some children continue to suffer. If the physical or behavioral stress symptoms do not diminish after a few weeks or if the symptoms become worse, it is time to seek professional help. A mental health professional can assist you and your child in coping with stress reactions.

How to Reassure Your Child

When children experience a significant trauma or major loss, there is a range of feelings and behaviors, which are normal, and there are also specific ways in which parents can support their children. Whether the trauma is a natural one, such as a pandemic, fire, tornado, earthquake, or flood, or whether the trauma is a personal loss such as a death in the family, children may often respond with similar kinds of emotions to those experienced by adults, such as fear or anxiety, and they need additional support from people who love them.

When a family or a community is faced with devastating trauma, many parents worry more about their children than they do about themselves. During the period of transition and readjustment, you may ask questions such as "Do my children feel stressed in the same ways that I do? What is normal behavior for children who have been through an experience like the recent disaster? What can I say or do to help my children through the experience in the most positive way?"

There are a few guidelines, which may be helpful for parents who want to encourage their children to express their feelings and talk about their concerns.

First of all, it is important to remember that children grieve losses and react to stress in different ways than adults do. They are not just miniature adults... they see and think and feel different things, depending on their developmental ages, their personalities, how they perceived the threat of what has occurred, and a number of other factors. For example, a child who experienced a tragedy and was immediately protected and comforted by a parent has a far different reaction than a child who was terrified and had to negotiate the experience on their own. Supporting the two children would require different kinds and different amounts of reassurance because the children's perceptions were so different.

To use a different example, an infant or toddler doesn't think about disasters, and can't conceive of what the term even means. But the child can feel the emotions of the people around him or her, see the distress on their faces, and sense the loss. What the child needs most from a parent is increased holding, touching, and being reassured in primary ways like rocking, singing, and just being close. On the other hand, a child between the ages of 5 and 7 understands somewhat more, but is still unable to grasp the totality of what has occurred. This child may express feelings directly through tears, anger, or fear of another disaster, or express feelings indirectly by having nightmares, temper tantrums, being afraid of the dark, being reluctant to go to school, or in some other way.

It is most helpful if a parent can accept such expressions and reassure the child that such feelings are normal, that the child is not a failure, and that dealing with change and stressful feelings are different for everyone. Reassuring a child that you understand is the first step in helping the child to rebuild independence and self-esteem.

Opening the door to talk about feelings associated with the disaster can be done in a number of ways. Sharing your own thoughts and feelings can be one way of beginning. For example: "Today I heard some people talking and they were pretty worried about having another disaster. I worry too sometimes, and I wonder how you feel? How are you feeling? Are you worried? What is one of your biggest worries?" Using questions that begin with HOW, WHAT, WHY, WHEN, WHERE, often encourage a child to explore feelings more than questions that can be answered by "yes" or "no". For example: "How did you feel when the disaster occurred? What did you think was happening? Why do you think it happened? When were you most worried?"

Some children will be eager to talk and others might find it easier to draw or act out their feelings. Sometimes "practicing" what your family will do helps children to be in touch with feelings that they would otherwise deny. Acting out scenarios of how the family will find safe places and take care of each other is reassuring and helps a child feel more in control of the outcome. Inviting a child to help assemble a family kit to be ready should a flood, tornado, or earthquake occur and deciding where to put the flashlights, batteries and the radio is therapeutic for everyone. If a disaster is more like a pandemic, parents can be creative and respond with supportive activities. In every case, parents or caregivers know their children best, and they can be creative and respond with supportive activities like singing, playing games, or sharing stories.

Some children, despite your encouragement, may choose not to talk or express their feelings. This is OK, too. There is no rule that says that you have to talk... lack of talking does not mean lack of feelings: it may indicate, rather, a need for time.

We all work out things in our own timing. Just leaving the door open and encouraging the child is a gift. Reassure your child that your child is doing a very good job of growing up and being a great kid. In the end, some children will have cried, others will have few or no tears. Children can feel confused and misunderstood if they are forced to talk. Believe that your child is doing exactly as your child needs to for himself or herself. There is no question that your child is doing the very best that your child can to discover outlets for how he or she feels.

Children, following trauma or loss, often ask many questions. Questions may be around practical things like: "Will we stay where we are now? What will happen if we get separated and I can't find you?" Sometimes there will questions about life and death. Most often, beneath these questions are two or three basic questions: "Am I safe? Will I survive? Will we be OK?" The best thing to do is to always answer your child's questions as directly and as honestly as possible. "Yes, we will try to stay here. If we get separated there will be someone who will help you. I will be there as soon as I can." It is also important to reassure the child as much as possible that he or she will be safe and that "we will be okay". The words are not as important as the tone. Your child will tell by your tone and reassurance whether or not there is reason to be afraid.

A common way that children deal with stress following a trauma is to regress to behaviors or feelings of earlier times. When children regress, they often temporarily lose their most recently acquired developmental accomplishment. For example, if they were recently toilet trained, they may suddenly have many "accidents". If they've recently started sleeping with the light out, they may be afraid and want the light on at night. It is important to gently accept the behavior and reassure the child that it is okay to do this again. "Everyone gets worried in different ways and soon you'll be able to sleep in the dark, again." An important message that you can give your child is to reassure her that other people are working hard to deal with the disaster and that she doesn't have to fix anything: "You don't have to worry about fixing these problems. There are lots of hard-working, smart people working together to make things better. We will be okay."

Finally, a traumatic event such as a major disaster increases the importance of the parents in providing additional support for their children. In an environment of care, love, and acceptance, children tend to be able to adjust and to grow up feeling good about their ability to adapt in a changing environment. This is not to say children do not experience fear or anxiety related to the event. However, children are less threatened in a nurturing environment that respects them as unique, worthy, and able to cope.

Should you, as a parent, feel continuing concern that your child is not making a positive adjustment, be sure to ask for help. Talking to other parents whom you trust, to your child's teachers, perhaps to a counselor who specializes in children's development, can help you decide if there is a problem that needs outside help. There are many loving people who are well trained, available, and eager to help. You know your children better than anyone else; trust your instincts about what you and your family need.

How to Listen so That Your Child Will Talk to You

Perhaps there's no more important skill for a parent to possess - especially following a traumatic period -- than the skill of being able to listen in such a way that you actually help your child talk with you about her experience and about her feelings and concerns. All of the approaches mentioned in this section are known and practiced by most parents when things are going along smoothly. At times of difficulty, crisis or trauma -- such as a recent disaster -- when we adults ourselves are under extraordinary stress it's sometimes easy to forget these methods. This section offers a brief review of some of the most important things you can do to help your child talk with you. As you read this section, you may not read anything that is truly new to you or to your way of listening to your child. We suggest that you just use what follows as a kind of review checklist to remind yourself of some of these important ways of helping your child during this difficult period.

Basic to your child's willingness to explore his fearful thoughts and stressful feelings with you is his trusting recognition of your love and acceptance of him. Remind yourself of the importance of actively letting him know that you love and accept him. This includes, of course, saying "I love you", or "I really like being with you" and any other words and phrases that let your child know of your respect and liking for him.

Touching is also a simple and powerful way of communicating these important feelings. Hugging, patting, and stroking are all very valuable ways of letting your child know just how special he is to you.

Careful listening has to begin with your genuine interest in whatever it is your child is experiencing and feeling. From this feeling of sincere interest we can move to letting our children know that we want to hear them; we can convey to them a recognition of our deep interest in their experience and in their thoughts and feelings.

We all can tell when someone is really listening to us -- we read this in what they do as well as in what they say and how they say it. We can use this awareness to build a checklist for ourselves as we watch the ways we encourage our children to share themselves with us. A beginning list would include four reminders; you'll be able to add others that will seem natural to you. Four points to begin with are:
First:
Looking at your child with attention and interest; making and keeping direct eye contact;

Second:
Making sure that each day includes some time when you let yourself stop everything else you're doing and just listen to your child;

Third:
Using encouraging expressions like "mm-hmm" "and what did you do then?" to let your child know that you're truly following what she's saying;

Fourth:
Just allowing your child to tell her story in her own way and in her own words and with her own sense of timing.

Three other specific points might be helpful reminders for you. These are: using wait-time, using "I" messages and avoiding defense-provoking questions. Let's review these briefly.

When you ask your child a question, how long do you wait for an answer before you repeat yourself, ask her another question, or offer a series of suggestion. Wait-time, as its name implies, refers to the period of time you wait for an answer after asking your child a question. If you are like many parents, you may allow very little time sometimes only one second - for your child to begin her answer to your question. And then, after a child makes her response, many parents are apt to wait even less time than they did prior to her answer to repeat what the child said or to rephrase it or to ask another question. If you think this describes you at times, you may decide to experiment with increasing your wait-time. When you ask a question, try waiting longer for an answer than you typically do. We know that waiting even five to seven seconds can sometimes produce some rather profound changes in the child's answer. You may even want to try counting your wait-time seconds by saying to yourself "one-1000, two-1000, three-1000, four-1000" and so forth in order to get a more clear sense of just how much time you're allowing your child to respond.

As your child learns that you're not going to hurry right on with another question or comment, you'll discover that he will begin to add to his answer, to say a bit more and to become even more exploring of his own thoughts and feelings.

Sharing yourself with your child by using "I" messages can be one of the most useful ways of enriching family communication. Recall that this method uses "I" as a starting point and includes a genuine expression and report of your own feelings and your own experience at that moment. When, for instance, your child says, "I really like being with you, Daddy." Instead of responding with "That's nice, son." try saying something like, "When I hear you say that I feel really good. I feel the same way about being with you."

Our final reminder is to try to avoid questioning in a way that puts your child on the defensive. An easy pit-fall here is to slip into the habit of asking only "Why" questions such as "Why did you do that?" or "Why did you go there?" "Why" questions usually make most of us try to think of reasons or explanations and can easily put us on the defensive and make us close down our communication. The same is certainly true with our children. One way of helping your child talk more freely is to rephrase these questions in a softer, more exploring way. Instead of "why did you do that?" you might try something like "say more about what you were thinking when you did that..." Instead of "Why are you still frightened?" you can probably hear much more from your child by asking "What things seem most frightening to you now about the fire (flood, etc.)?"

Reminding yourself to employ these caring ways of listening can bring rich rewards to you and to your child. Careful listening is one of the most important ways to build a strong, positive relationship with your child following a disaster.

This kind of listening also affords your child the opportunity to listen to herself in constructive and less stressful ways. Your way of listening to her can help her develop ways of listening to her own inner voices in more loving, self-accepting ways that will significantly reduce her disastershock.

How to Use Art to Help Your Child Cope with Stress

Art is a great way to help your child deal with disaster related stress. This section describes a few simple art activities you can do right at home. The idea is to give your child the opportunity to gain back mastery by using your child's natural ability to create and be spontaneous. You're going to need some simple materials. For the first project, the "Me Box", (see Figure 1) you're going to need to scour the house for some old magazines, some glue and scissors, and find a box of any size that is particularly appealing to your child.

It can be small or large. Round, oatmeal boxes are particularly fun for this project and you might have one lying around. Have the child sort through the magazines for pictures that represent the inside of themselves and for pictures that will represent feelings and experiences on the outside of themselves. For example, wishes, or secrets and private thoughts or dreams may be put on the inside of the box. External things like places to go, pictures of things to do, or things that are particularly fun may be put on the outside of the box.

Figure 1. The "Me Box"

Another aspect of this "Me Box" is to go on a treasure hunt to find things on the inside of the house and the outside of the house to add to the box. Photographs, pieces of fabric, or special trinkets that are particularly important to the child, may be put in the inside of the box. Things that you find on the outside of the house that are particular treasures in the garden or on the street and that may reflect ways the world around the child have changed may be added to the outside of the box. In this way your child creates what we call a "Me Box" that completely projects who your child is in his or her world.

An extension of the "Me Box" idea is to put the inside images and outside images on a piece of folded paper. An 18" by 14" padded paper that you can find in a local drugstore will be fine for this. Gluing images on to boxes or papers is particularly fun for kids at almost any age. Glitter, feather, ribbons, and other found decorative items can be added to embellish the box or paper collage project and make it truly special and expressive.

If you have some drawing or painting materials around the house or you can get ahold of them easily, you might try the next project called "A Once Upon a Time Fairy Tale Drawing or Painting" (see Figure 2). Begin by having your child choose a special place for working, such as a table, and choose the art medium that he or she likes best. Tell your child that this art project is to be about a kingdom and suggest these following words. "Once upon a time, there was a kingdom where there was a hurricane (flood, earthquake, etc.)" and then let your child fill in the rest of the story by drawing or painting images of what your child thinks happened in this kingdom. Encourage your child to put animals and imagined or real characters in the drawing or painting.

Figure 2. A Once Upon a Time Fairy Tale Drawing or Painting

The picture does not have to be representational of the child's actual experience of the disaster. It provides, through fantasy, a safe way for your child to talk about his or her concerns. As this fantasy kingdom is created, you might suggest characters that you think could be helpful, such as doctors or nurses, policemen or parents, or even fantasy characters who could be particularly helpful in the fantasy kingdom situation of a disaster (see Figure 3). Another constructive way to make pictures is by tearing up pieces of colored paper or magazines to build pictures by gluing them on to a piece of paper (see Figure 4). Simple shapes like circles or triangles can be used. You can also make a 3-D Play Doh or paper mache sculpture of a guardian spirit or a protective character (see Figure 5).

Figure 3. Helpful Characters in the Fantasy Kingdom

Figure 4. Making a Picture by Tearing Up and Gluing Pieces of Paper

A paper mache sculpture may be made by using a balloon for the shape of the body. Blow up the balloon, tie it up, and simply put your newspaper strips dipped in the glue onto the balloon and in that way form the basic body. Later when the paper mache figure has dried, you can pop the balloon with a pin. You can build up the characters' shape and clothing (such as wings and capes and other details), and face, hands and paws by adding little pieces of tissue paper or little pieces of newspaper dipped in the glue. Fingers get very messy with this project and so does the table, so you will need to cover the whole work area with newspaper, and maybe have your child wear a smock. The paper mache figure will need to dry overnight. After it's dry, your child will want to paint or decorate it so that it becomes truly your child's own. You might find that your child has turned the sculpture piece into a monster or a scary figure instead of a protective guardian figure. The process of transforming fears by making them through art materials or by playing them out is a natural coping mechanism of children experiencing stress. You might take this opportunity to encourage your child to seek an outlet to explore feelings and to stay safe at the same time by exploring the scary idea together and then by thinking of alternative comforting characters that maybe you enjoyed as a child. By making the comforting character in a 3-d sculpture or paper mache and decorating it, it can be kept in the child's room to chase away scary monsters or nightmares. It can become, in essence, a friend for the child.

Children are naturally curious about their worlds and you can work with your child to make an earthquake (flood, etc.) art journal that will contain the child's own special experience of the disaster (see Figure 6). The art journal can be made in an art pad with a spiral edge and could include sections with tabs for actual newspaper clippings, places where drawings or poems can

Figure 5. 3-D Guardian Spirit or Protective Figure

be put in about ideas they have had about the disaster. Another section could include ways the world is being put back together in a positive direction. For instance, how people help each other and ideas that your child might have for ways that they can help their family or others. Another section of the art journal could be called "wishes". This could include drawings or lists of wishes that the child has for himself or herself, for the family, or for other people that your child has heard about or knows. Another section could be maps or safety routes of the house, of ways to stay safe and of plans that can be made to stay safe in situations such as a disaster.

Encouraging the child to decorate the outside of the cover for this art journal is important. Painting or drawing that conveys what it was like for them and that they are OK after the earthquake is important. Children need to know that they were successful and survivors in living through a disaster that affected us all. They need to be allowed to review their feeling of being a part of this part of history. The art journal is a way to let them express their feelings concerning the disaster while participating in a constructive art project that requires mastery. Working closely together on this project with your children can be comforting. In fact, the whole family could participate and it can be a family project.

We hope you'll find these suggestions useful and are sure that your children will elaborate on the ideas in their own unique and very creative ways. Art is a useful way not only to express feelings and to get them out, but also to transform them through uses of media in stress-

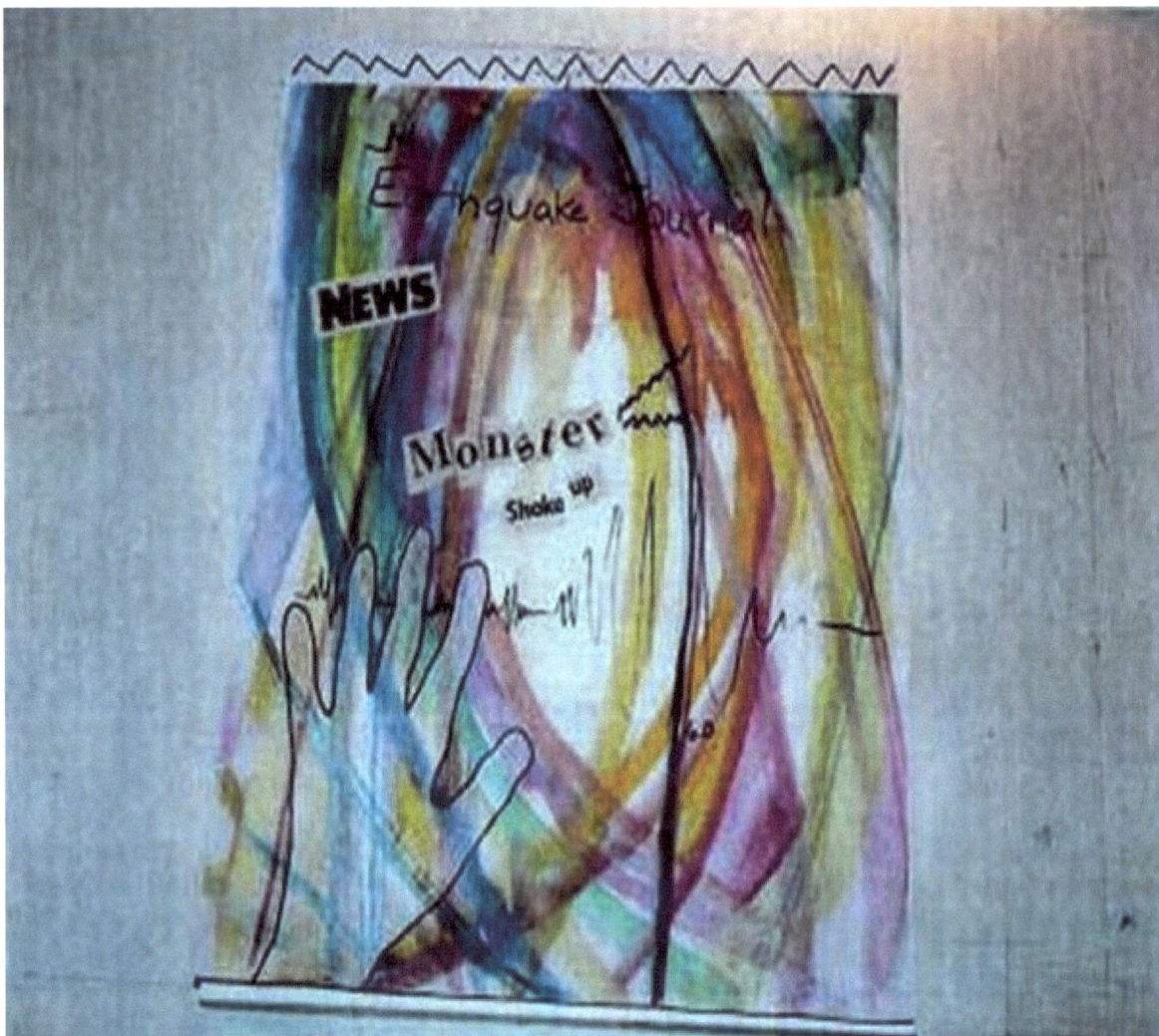

Figure 6.   A Disaster Art Journal

reducing ways. Active participation in art helps put a temporal perspective on personal experience. For example, a drawing about a disaster is something about an event that happened in the past and it allows us a chance to see in a concrete, visual way that, in fact, the stressful event is over. It allows children to go on to consider what life will be like for now and in the future. Allowing children to do the natural work of childhood by creating in art media, by building up and tearing down, by constructing and exploring, by interpreting with their hands and their eyes, permits them to express their physical and emotional world. Art is a great idea for anyone, and easy to do at home. And we suggest that it's a lot of fun!

How to Help your Child to Relax: Ten Methods

This section describes 10 effective methods that you can use to help your child to relax and cope with tension, anxiety, or fear related to disasters.

Method 1: Be Relaxed Yourself

This is the most important method for helping your child. If you are feeling stressed, your child may sense this, and feel stressed too. If you are feeling anxious and tense, how can you expect your child to feel relaxed? By being relaxed yourself you will be a role-model of calmness for your child. Your child will be likely to copy your relaxed behavior. You can learn to relax by trying the 10 coping methods for adults described in Part I of this book.

Method 2: Deep Breathing

This is the relaxation method of breathing slowly and deeply. Show your child how to do it by breathing slowly and deeply yourself. Breathe slowly in through your nose for 2 seconds, hold your breath for 2 seconds, then breathe out slowly for 2 seconds. Repeat this several times so your child gets the idea, then have your child breathe along with you. Ask your child to silently count each breath in. Together with your child practice deep breathing for 20 breaths in and out. Then stop and talk about how relaxed you feel. To help your child concentrate ask your child to focus on counting each breath in.

Another way to help your child focus on deep breathing is to ask your child to close his or her eyes while practicing. Having your child practice deep breathing while having a warm bath may also help your child to relax. If your child is 10 or younger, make a game of Deep Breathing by asking your child to imagine being a Kung Fu Master practicing relaxation, or a Deep-Sea Diver or Astronaut conserving air. If your child feels any discomfort practicing Deep Breathing, try another method. If your child is able to practice Deep Breathing, instruct your child to practice Deep Breathing whenever he or she feels tense.

Method 3: Muscle Relaxation

This is the relaxation method of getting your child to relax her or his muscles. It is difficult to feel tense if your muscles are feeling relaxed.

There are 2 ways to teach your child to relax muscles. First, ask your child to think the word "relax" while having a warm bath. Later, after the bath ask your child to think the word "relax" and imagine he is lying in the warm bath. Second, you can show your child how to relax muscles by tensing them all up for 5 seconds, then suddenly relaxing them while thinking the word "relax". Demonstrate this for your child by sitting in a chair with your feet together and your knees together. Place your hands on the sides of your thighs so that you are pressing your knees together. Now, push your legs together and push your knees together until you feel pressure in your muscles. Keep pushing for 5 seconds, and then let your muscles go limp. Think:

"relax" as you let go. Imagine you are relaxed and limp like a rag doll. Notice the contrast between your muscles being tense and being relaxed. If you feel pain at any time, stop.

Now do it together with your child. Talk to your child about how relaxed your muscles feel after going limp. This is a good relaxation technique for your child to try whenever your child is feeling tense and is at home or alone.

Method 4: Imagining Your Favorite Activity

This is the relaxation method of having your child imagine a favorite activity whenever your child starts to feel tense. Show your child how to do this by sitting down with your child and practicing it yourself. Say: "I'm going to show you a good way to relax by imagining a favorite activity. My favorite activity is..." (And here you should tell your child what your favorite activity is. For you it might be lying on the beach, sitting with a favorite cat or dog, watching a favorite sport, anything at all). Then close your eyes and imagine your favorite activity for about 30 seconds. When you open your eyes, tell your child what you imagined and how relaxed it made you feel. Next, ask your child what her favorite activity is that she would like to imagine. Ask her to close her eyes and imagine it for 30 seconds. When the 30 seconds is up, ask her what she imagined and whether she feels more relaxed. Congratulate her on how well she did her exercise. Next, both of you should practice imagining your favorite activity together. After 30 seconds, talk about how imagining your favorite activities made you feel relaxed. Tell your child that whenever she feels tense, she can relax by imagining her favorite activity.

Method 5: Thought-Stopping

This is a relaxation method that your child can use when he has learned methods 2, 3, and 4. Thought-Stopping combines Deep Breathing, Muscle Relaxation, and Imagining Your Favorite Activity. Whenever your child begins to have an unpleasant thought about the disaster, or anything at all, he can turn off the unpleasant thought by using Thought- Stopping.

Tell your child: "The moment you start to think an unpleasant thought, imagine someone is shouting the word STOP. Then take a slow, deep breath, think the word Relax, let your muscles go limp like a rag doll and think of your favorite activity as you continue to breathe slowly and deeply." Show your child how to do this by describing aloud each step as you do it. Say: "I'm going to show you how to do Thought-Stopping. OK, here goes. First, I'm starting to think of an unpleasant thought about the disaster. It's very unpleasant so I want to turn it off using Thought-Stopping. Second, I'm imagining someone yelling: "Stop". Third, I take a slow deep breath (Parent: breathe in and then out slowly and noisily). Fourth, I think the word "Relax" and let my muscles go limp. Fifth, as I breathe slowly and deeply ten times, I think of my favorite activity." When you are finished, tell your child how relaxed this method makes you feel. Next, ask your child to tell you what the 5 steps of Thought-Stopping are. Correct any errors. When your child can describe the 5 steps, ask him to describe them as he practices each one. Once more, correct any errors he makes. Congratulate him on each step he does well. Next, ask him to practice the 5 steps of Thought-Stopping silently. Have him practice Thought-Stopping in front of you 3 or 4 times (about I minute each time). Talk with him about how relaxed he feels after trying Thought-Stopping. Tell your child that Thought-Stopping is a method he can use every time he has an unpleasant thought that makes him feel tense or afraid.

Method 6: Being Your own Coach

This is the method of relaxing by thinking encouraging thoughts to yourself. You give yourself a "pep talk" the way a good coach might give a "pep talk" to boost a team's spirits before a big game.

Talk to your child this way: "Each time you start to feel tense or afraid, pretend you are the coach of your favorite team and give yourself a pep talk. Think to yourself positive thoughts like:

"You can do it."

"Relax, everything will be OK."

"Stay calm."

"I can handle this."

"Breathe slowly and take it easy."

"I've succeeded before."

"My parents will be proud of me."

Show your child how to do this by doing it yourself. Say: "Watch me try it. OK, I'm starting to feel tense so I know this is a sign that I should start being my own coach and give myself a pep talk. Here goes... I can handle this ... Relax ... I can do it.... Breathe slowly and take it easy ... Stay calm... I've succeeded before.... My family will be proud of me...". Share with your child how being your own coach makes you feel more relaxed. Next, ask your child to describe aloud each step in Being Your Own Coach as she tries it in front of you. Correct any errors and congratulate her on the parts she did well. Next, ask your child to silently practice being her own coach in front of you for 2 minutes. Talk about how it went and ask her what pep talk statements she gave herself. Congratulate her on being a good coach. Tell her to try this whenever she feels tense. You might like to write down on a small filing card some of the positive coaching statements that your child would like to use. Tell her that she can carry this in a pocket and read it whenever she needs a reminder of what her positive coaching statements are.

Method 7: The "Yes... But" Technique

This is the relaxation method of pointing out to your child something positive about a situation he thinks is negative. If your child says: "I am afraid you will catch the coronavirus and die", you can say: "It is unlikely I will catch the coronavirus because I am using social distancing and using hand sanitizer. The majority of persons who get sick with the coronavirus recover. So if I did get sick there would be a very good chance I would recover and be ok." If your child says: "The earthquake (fire, etc.) killed people," you can say: "Yes, that's true, but many were not killed and most people were not harmed at all." If your child says: "Terrorists are going to destroy our city", you can say "Terrorists did attack one city but there have been no further attacks and we are safe here." If your child says: "I'm afraid there will be another flood (tornado, etc.) and I won't know where to find you", say: "Yes, there might possibly be another disaster, but even if we were separated for a little while, we would find you and be together" (and then you might discuss a family plan for how you all would get together if you were temporarily separated).

To use this "Yes... But" approach, you acknowledge that the fearful event that your child has described is partly true, then you point out something positive that he has overlooked. This is a way to give your child hope and reduce his tension.

Method 8: Mutual Storytelling

This is an approach that is especially useful with young children under age 10. Ask your child to tell you a story about the disaster. If her story has a scary ending, you can retell the story, but give it a happy ending. Put your child's favorite hero into the story and describe how the hero helps your child to cope successfully. For boys you might say: "...and Spiderman together with you lead the other children to safety. You point out a telephone to Spiderman and together you phone your parents. Spiderman says to you: "You have great courage. I'm lucky to have you at my side". For girls you might say: "Together with Wonder Woman you leave school and walk home. Wonder Woman congratulates you on how brave you are and you get home and we are all together with Wonder Woman sitting at your side." These are just brief examples to give you the idea. You can make up longer stories in which your child's hero helps your child and congratulates your child on his or her bravery.

Method 9: Rewarding Bravery and Calmness

This is the method of noticing those moments when your child acts in a brave or calm manner and then praising your child. if your child has been very anxious, wait for a moment when she is quietly watching TV (or calmly doing some other activity) and say: I'm so proud of how you are relaxing." If she has been afraid to go to school and be away from you, but does go once or twice, say: "I am so proud of the way you went to school today. You were very brave." Do not make a big fuss over the fact that your child has been acting tense, anxious or fearful. These feelings are natural. Look for even tiny behaviors of your child that show calmness and praise them: "I am so proud of the way you didn't cry when I dropped you off at school today. You are a very brave girl." Your child values your praise and will want to act even braver and calmer.

Method 10: Books for Children on Dealing with Fear

You can help your child to relax by giving him a book to read that has a story about other children who cope effectively with fear and scary situations.

Some books for children that deal with children's fears in general are:

Crist, James J. (2004). *What to Do When You're Scared and Worried: A Guide for Kids*. Minneapolis, MN: Free Spirit Publishing.

Guanci, Anne Marie (2007). *David and the Worry Beast: Helping Children Cope with Anxiety*. Far Hills, NJ: Horizon Press.

Membling, Carl & Johnson, John E. (1971). *What's in the Dark?* New York, NY: Parents' Magazine Press.

Meredith, Dawn (2014). *12 Annoying Monsters: Self-talk for Kids with Anxiety*. Hazelbrook, NSW: MoshPit Publishing.

Moses, Melissa & MacEachern, Alison (2015). *Alex and the Scary Things: A Story to Help Children Who Have Experienced Something Scary*. London, UK: Jessica Kingsley Publishers

Viorst, Judith (1987). *My Mama Says They're Aren't Any Zombies, Ghosts, Vampires, Creatures, Demons, Monsters, Fiends, Goblins, or Things.* New York, NY: Simon & Shuster

and two books dealing with children's fears about death are:

Buscaglia, Leo (1982). *The Fall of Freddie the Leaf: A Story of Life for All Ages.* Thorofare,NJ: Slack Incorporated.

Rowland, Joanna & Baker, Thea (2017). The memory box: A book about grief. MN: Sparkhouse Family Publishing.

Thomas, Pat & Harker, Leslie (2001). *I Miss You: A First Look at Death.* Hauppauge, NY: Barron's Educational Series.

Your bookstore website or local bookstore or library will have many other books that can help your child cope with fear. You should feel free to ask your librarian or bookstore manager for suggestions and then read the books yourself to see if they are suitable for your child.

You may wish to try several of these methods to help your child relax. Choose the ones that you feel the most confident about and try them first. But remember the most important one: that you need to be relaxed yourself first.

Method 11: Engaging in Fun Activities

Often during a disaster, to be safe it is important to have everyone stay at home. This is particularly so during a pandemic such as the coronavirus pandemic. Parents are often at a loss as to how to help their children deal with boredom and the inability to go outside. Karen Wood Peyton has written a useful book called: <u>Families on the Home Front: Activities to encourage your child's development and growth during a pandemic</u>. The book (at this writing) is available free on Amazon. This book contains over 100 activities you can do with your children. The book is divided into 9 sections:

Social Activities Around the Home (e.g. Have a family game night; Have a family costume party).

Gross Motor Activities Around the House (e.g. have a family scavenger hunt; Have a family workout).

Fine Motor Activities Around the House (e.g. Play Board Games; Play with Blocks).

Fun Food Activities (e.g. Do a Blind Taste Test; Host an International Dinner Night).

Learning Time (e.g. Organize a Show and Tell; Go to the "Museum").

Lights, Camera, Action! (e.g. Do a Talent Show; Watch Old Home Movies).

Make and Create Activities (e.g. Build a Fort; Make and Illustrate a Book).

Outdoor Activities (e.g. Collect Leaves; Play Freeze Tag).

Self-Care Activities (e.g. Nutrition; Hygiene; Sleep).

The advantage of engaging in these activities is that many of them involve the entire family in doing something that is fun and educational and a distraction from stress.

Method 12: Family Meeting

When there is tension in a family, children are affected. Holding a Family Meeting can be an effective way to manage family tensions and differences, e.g. family members arguing over what tv show to watch; disagreements about meals or bedtimes; any matter where a family member is in disagreement with other family members. A Family Meeting is a meeting attended by all family members who sit in a circle. The Family Meeting is typically held once a week (or shorter time period if disagreements are frequent, e.g. twice a week) and for a limited time period (1 hour for a large family, 30 minutes for a small family).

A parent begins by describing the basic rules for the Family Meeting:

a) Everyone gets a chance to speak.

b) There is no name-calling, swearing, or shouting allowed.

c) Each family member gets to speak in turn for 2-3 minutes about some matter of concern.

d) There is an emphasis on trying to understand each family member's concerns and finding a solution to any problems.

e) A Speaker's Permit, like a stuffed animal or ball, is given to the speaker to hold as a reminder to everyone that only the person holding the object is permitted to speak.

After the family member with the Speaker's Permit has shared their concern for a maximum of 3 minutes (a family member should be the timekeeper), the Speaker's Permit passes to the person on the right who may then speak for up to 3 minutes if they wish, or they may pass the Speaker's Permit to the next person to the right. This turn-taking in speaking continues until the allotted time for the Family Meeting is up. The following example of a Family Meeting is for a family where a mother and father have requested a Family Meeting to discuss an argument between the son (age 10) and the daughter (age 8).

Mother: I would like to begin our Family Meeting. Please remember the rules: we all need to speak in a respectful manner: no shouting, name-calling or swearing. Our goal to hear the concerns and point of view of each family member and to try and think of solutions to any problems.

Father: We are one family and what affects one of us affects all of us. Remember only the person holding the Speaker's Permit – we will use this ball – is allowed to speak and can talk for up to 3 minutes.

Mother: (handing ball to daughter). OK, why don't you begin and tell us about any concerns you have.

Daughter: (holding ball) Whenever I watch TV, he (pointing at brother) comes in and changes the channel.

Son: No, I don't!

Mother: Son, you have to wait your turn. Only the person with the ball can speak. Daughter, please continue.

Daughter: My favorite show is on Wednesday at 5 pm and yesterday while I was watching it he grabbed the TV remote and changed the channel to watch some police show. I asked him to change it back and he just yelled at me to go away.

Mother: Thank you for sharing your feelings. That must have been upsetting for you. Now pass the ball to your brother. Son, it's now your turn to talk.

Son: It's not fair! She's just watching cartoons. My show is about sports and it's on at the same time and it is more important. And I am older!

Mother: Thank you for sharing your feelings. Please pass the ball to father. Father it's your turn.

Father: I think we need a solution that works for both of you. I recommend that we record both programs each week and then each of you can play it back at a different time. (passes ball to mother).

Mother: I can see a problem: what if both want to play their program back at the same time? (passes ball to daughter).

Daughter: What if we took turns? I could watch my show on one day and he could watch his show on another day (passes ball to brother).

Son: I could write the days on a piece of paper and put our names on different days so we know whose turn it is (passes ball to Mother).

Mother: Our time for the Family meeting is almost up. This sounds like a good solution! Does everyone agree that we try it? (everyone agrees). When we have our next Family Meeting we can talk about how it went.

The advantage of holding a Family Meeting is that it allows family issues to be shared in a structured manner that prevents any one family member from monopolizing the conversation. There are other ways to hold a Family Meeting. A useful book on holding family meetings of this kind is: Family Meeting Handbook: Here for Each Other, Hearing Each Other.

PART 3: ADDITIONAL BOOKS, VIDEOS, AND INTERNET RESOURCES

Two books for parents/guardians on dealing with children's fears are:

Chansky, Tamar E. (2004). *Freeing Your Child from Anxiety: Powerful, Practical Solutions to Overcome Your Child's Fears, Worries, and Phobias.* New York, NY: Broadway Books.

Mellonie, Bryan & Ingpen, Robert (1983). *Lifetimes: The Beautiful Way to Explain Death to Children.* Melbourne, VI: Michelle Anderson Publishing.

Just for Adults

Lattanzi-Licht, Marcia E. & Doka, Kenneth J. (2003). *Coping With Public Tragedy (Living With Grief).* New York, NY: Hospice Foundation of America.

Saari, Salli (2005). *A Bolt From the Blue: Coping with Disasters and Acute Traumas*. London, UK: Jessica Kingsley Publishers.

Additional Internet Resources: Websites and Videos

Below are listed some websites describing ways to help children cope with stress.

Helping children through crisis: Tips for parents and caregivers (from MercyCorps)
https://www.mercycorps.org/helping-children-through-crisis-tips-parents-and-caregivers

Helping Children Cope with Crisis: Just for Parents (from *Eunice Kennedy Shriver* National Institute of Child Health and Human Development)
https://www.nichd.nih.gov/publications/pubs/cope_with_crisis_book/Pages/sub11.aspx

Helping kids during crisis (from American School Counselor Association)
https://www.schoolcounselor.org/school-counselors-members/professional-development/2016-webinar-series/learn-more/helping-kids-during-crisis

Responding to a crisis (from the School Mental Health Project at the University of California, Los Angeles)
http://smhp.psych.ucla.edu

Age–related reactions to a traumatic event (from The National Child Traumatic Stress Network)
http://www.nctsn.org/sites/default/files/assets/pdfs/age_related_reactions_to_a_traumaticevent.pdf

School safety and crisis (from National Association of School Psychologists)
https://www.nasponline.org/resources-and-publications/resources/school-safety-and-crisis

The child survivor of traumatic stress
 http://users.umassmed.edu/Kenneth.Fletcher/kidsurv.html

Coping with emotions after a disaster
http://www.apa.org/helpcenter/recoveringdisasters.aspx

Videos

Helping children cope with crisis situations (School psychologist Ted Feinberg discusses how to help children cope with crisis situations).
http://monkeysee.com/helping-children-cope-with-crisis-situations/

Helping your child cope with media coverage of disasters (from Disaster and Community Crisis Center, University of Missouri)
https://www.youtube.com/watch?v=BqYZMYqsLqQ

Helping children cope with a natural disaster (Dr. Ryan Denney, a licensed psychologist, gives tips on how parents can help children cope with natural disasters).
https://www.youtube.com/watch?v=i93fhVdYVFw

Talking to your Kids about Disasters, Death, Dying and Tragic News (Important information about helping kids cope with grief and troubling news from Dr. Bob Hilt, director of psychiatric emergency services at Seattle Children's Hospital).
https://www.youtube.com/watch?v=d3v4ZyirhIs

Conclusion

You may wish to try several of these methods to help your child relax. Choose the ones that you feel the most confident about and try them first. But remember the most important one: that you first need to be relaxed yourself. If, after reading this book and trying several of the methods on it, you find that you or your child are still very stressed, we strongly recommend that you consult a qualified mental health professional.

About the Authors

Dr. Valerie Appelton

Dr. Appleton held an EdD in Educational Psychology from the University of San Francisco. She was one of the first doctoral interns to work in the University of San Francisco's Center for Child and Family Development Community Counseling Center. Dr. Appleton was a professor and Dean at Eastern Washington University in Cheney, Washington where she taught art therapy. She was also a mentor to many other art therapists who praised her unique teaching style. Her publications include: "Avenues of Hope: Art Therapy and the Resolution of Trauma", "An Art Therapy Protocol for the Medical Trauma Setting", "Team building in educational settings", "School crisis intervention: Building effective crisis management teams", and "Using art in group counseling with Native American youth." We are sad to report her untimely death in 2005. We are grateful to Dr. Appleton for her unique art therapy contribution to *Disastershock: How to Cope with the Emotional Stress of a Major Disaster.*

Dr. Brian Gerrard

Dr. Gerrard has a PhD in Sociology, from the University of New South Wales, Sydney, Australia and a PhD in Counseling Psychology, from the University of Toronto. Dr. Gerrard is an Emeritus faculty member of the University of San Francisco where he developed the masters MFT program and for 14 years served as MFT Coordinator. His orientation emphasizes an integration of family systems and problem-solving approaches. He is an experienced administrator and has been Chair of the USF Counseling Psychology Department three times. Currently, he is a member of the Board, University of San Francisco Center for Child and Family Development. The Center, co-founded by Dr. Gerrard, has for years managed the largest longest-running School-Based Family Counseling program of its type in the USA. Its Mission Possible Program has served more than 20,000 children and families in over 70 Bay area schools. Dr. Gerrard is also Chair of the Institute for School-Based Family Counseling and Symposium Director for the Oxford Symposium in School-Based Family Counseling. Currently, Dr. Gerrard is the Chief Administrative Officer and a Core Faculty member in the Western Institute for Social Research in Berkeley, California. He is senior editor of the book School-Based Family Counseling: An Interdisciplinary Practitioner's Guide (Routledge, 2019). Brian lives in Florida with his wife Olive, and more cats than he is willing to admit to.

Dr. Suzanne Giraudo

Suzanne Giraudo is Clinical Director of the Kalmanovitz Child Development Center Dept. of Pediatrics at California Pacific Medical Center. Dr. Giraudo is a psychologist working with children, adolescents, young adults and families and is active in the Medical Center's community health programs for over 25 years. In addition, she served on the Children and Families Commission for San Francisco for 12 years, is currently a member of the San Francisco Health Commission, is a trustee for DeMarillac Academy, on the advisory board of the University of San Francisco Health Professions. Dr. Giraudo has served on the boards of many non profits including Hamilton Family Center, Home Away From Homelessness and Catholic Charities, Coleman Advocates. She has given many presentations and participated in research in the fields, of education, health, child development and mental/behavioral health. Dr. Giraudo has been honored for her contributions with the Bank of America Local Heroes Award, The California Pacific Medical Center's Presidents Award and State Legislature 12th Assembly District Woman of the Year Award. Suzanne is a native San Franciscan and lives in the City with her husband.

Dr. Emily S. Girault

Dr. Girault has a PhD in Education from Stanford University. She is an Emerita faculty member in the Counseling Psychology department at the University of San Francisco. She taught courses in Group Counseling, Family Therapy, Personality, and Marital and Family Therapy Fieldwork. Dr. Girault was instrumental in developing the Counseling Psychology department's first off-campus marital and family therapy program in Palo Alto, California, which became the model for 4 other university off-campus programs. She was also co-founder of the University of San Francisco's Center for Child & Family Development. The Center has for years managed the largest longest-running School-Based Family Counseling program of its type in the USA. Its Mission Possible Program has served more than 20,000 children and families in over 70 Bay area schools. Dr. Girault was a founding member of the Institute for School-Based Family Counseling and played an important role in developing the Oxford Symposium in School-Based Family Counseling. Her co-authored article "Resource Personnel Workshops: A Team Approach to Educational Change" was published in the journal Social Education. Dr. Girault's research interests are in school-based family counseling, reflective teaching, and psychological type (Myers-Briggs Type Indicator).

Dr. Sue Linville Shaffer

Sue Linville Shaffer has an Ed.D. in Counseling Psychology from the University of San Francisco. She taught as a member of Adjunct Faculty at the University of San Francisco in the Graduate Program in Counseling Psychology from 1989 to 2018. Sue served as a consultant and bereavement specialist for Mid-Peninsula Pathways Hospice from 1990 to 2005, designing and facilitating hospice groups and providing bereavement in-service trainings to hospitals and nursing staffs in the Bay Area. Beginning in 2006, Sue became a consultant and clinical staff member at Kara, a nonprofit grief counseling agency providing grief and trauma support to individuals families and children in Palo Alto, California. She served as Director of Clinical Services for the agency from 2006 - 2020. Between 2011 and 2016 Sue participated in the Advanced Critical Incident Stress Management Team Bay Area (CISM), facilitating debriefings and crisis interventions in varied settings including schools, agencies, and workplaces Bay-Area wide. For 30 years Sue has maintained a clinical private practice in Menlo Park, California. She currently works with individuals, young adults, and families as well as facilitating groups for Young Widows and Widowers, Daughters Grieving Loss of Mother, and other groups related to healing following trauma and complicated loss.

Please feel free to give us feedback on *Disastershock: How to Cope with the Emotional Stress of a Major Disaster* by sending an e-mail to Dr. Brian Gerrard at gerrardb@usfca.edu. You can help us by telling us what approaches in the book helped you or your children the most and giving us suggestions on any ways to improve Disastershock.

www.ingramcontent.com/pod-product-compliance
Lightning Source LLC
Chambersburg PA
CBHW042059040426
42448CB00002B/63